Sheila Perey

Sheila Perey

Photography by
Ian Wallace

hamlyn

New Blooms

Over 40 fresh ideas for
seasonal flowers

Nick Green

First published in Great Britain in 2000
by Hamlyn, an imprint of Octopus Publishing Group Limited
2–4 Heron Quays, London E14 4JP

A CIP catalogue record of this book is available
from the British Library

ISBN 0 600 59751 2

Printed and bound in China

Creative Director: Keith Martin
Executive Art Editor: Mark Winwood
Designer: Ruth Hope
Executive Editor: Polly Manguel
Project Editor: Joanna Smith
Editors: Sharyn Conlan and Cathy Lowne
Indexer: Hilary Bird
Senior Production Controller: Katherine Hockley

Photographer: Ian Wallace
Additional Photography: Georgia Glynn Smith 28 (top right, top left,
bottom right), 78 (top right, top left, bottom right), 80 (top right, top
left, bottom left), 93–95, 98–9, 136–7

Flower Designer: Nick Green
All flowers supplied by:
Green
125 Shepherd's Bush Road
London W6 7LP

Contents

Introduction

There is a revolution going on now in the world of floristry and I am very excited by the challenges it presents. The traditional rules and guidelines have been replaced by contemporary modes of expression, a more natural and unstructured approach and the use of more basic elements, such as glass, metals and stones, in new ways. Ignore the stereotypes surrounding certain flowers and plants and discover their true essence. Flowers go in and out of fashion, but don't be afraid to express yourself as you like or to introduce some elements of fun in your flower arrangements – like the Easter Nest or the Valentine Orchid.

Another great thing about floristry at the moment is the wide choice of fresh flowers, foliage and plants that are easily available. Combine these with the profusion of wonderful containers, and it is possible for anyone to create stunning displays which complement their individual lifestyle. You dress to reflect your mood or personality, so why not choose your flowers in the same way? Your floral designs should reflect their settings, the occasion or the style and taste of the recipient.

Many designs today are very simple and unfussy. However, this does not mean that you cannot extend your creativity or personalize your creations with familiar and favourite things. It is important to express yourself through your designs – blaze your own trail! Concentrate on your theme and with a little hard work, imagination and a love of flowers the results will be fantastic.

Nick Green

spring

summer

autumn

winter

spring

▼ **Tulips** (*Tulipa*) In the garden, tulips flower in late spring, their sculptural flowers coming in all shapes and shades. The delicate colour of these green parrot tulips is offset by the shape of their quirky, fringed petals.

▼ **Miniature daffodils** (*Narcissus*) The essence of spring, simple, single-flowered miniature daffodils provide a welcome, but not overpowering, splash of bright colour in any arrangement. Their endearing faces will bring cheer on the darkest of days.

▲ **Irises** (*Iris*) The purple of these irises is a welcome addition to the yellows of spring flowers and their striking shape makes them great for contemporary designs. Buy them when they are just out of bud to make the most of them.

▼ **Grape hyacinths** (*Muscari*) Available in late spring, these little relatives of hyacinths add a splash of colour to small-scale arrangements. Their wonderful texture and uncompromising blue colour make them distinctive.

▼ **Lily-of-the-valley** (*Convallaria majalis*) The tiny, delicate white flowers work very well as a contrast to strong purples, making them great partners for flowers such as anemones. The leaves are an added bonus and the flowers have a rich, heady scent.

▲ **Narcissi** (*Narcissus*) More delicate than most daffodils, narcissi have one or more flowers per stem and give a cheerful lift to a simple spring arrangement. Their pale colour creates a stunning contrast to dark, shiny leaves.

Bluebell wood

A bluebell wood in spring is one of the most wonderful sights in nature. Here, fresh, cheerful bluebells are combined with bare twigs in a modest glass vase to create a pure and natural arrangement. The stems of the bluebells have a beauty of their own.

Time to make: 10 minutes

what you need
LARGE BUNCH OF BLUEBELLS
TWIGS
GLASS VASE
SECATEURS

preparation
1. Cut the twigs to fit the vase, selecting pieces that are straight at the base and slightly branched at the top.

building up
2. Take a few bluebell stems in your hand and add a twig or two to the bunch. Add a few more bluebells around the outside, then another twig. Continue to add to the bunch, arranging the twigs evenly among the bluebells, until the bunch is about the same diameter as the vase.

final touches
3. Cut the stems level at the base of the bunch, then insert the stems into the vase of water, taking care not to upset the carefully-arranged bunch. Use a little bleach in the water to keep it clear (see page 140).

variations
Many flowers combine well with bare twigs, but the best effects are had when the flowers grow naturally in woodland. Try hellebores, simple narcissi, snowdrops, violets or primroses. But remember not to pick the flowers from the wild.

Springtime gift

In France, lily-of-the-valley is a traditional gift for May Day, when the flowers are just beginning to emerge. Either grow them in a pot, then dig them up and wrap them with the roots still attached, or buy them as a bare-root crown, as here. The recipient can plant the lily-of-the-valley out in the garden after enjoying the flowers indoors. In this way, your exquisitely-fragrant gift will be remembered for much longer.

Time to make: 15 minutes

what you need
LILY-OF-THE-VALLEY CROWN
NATURAL RAFFIA
WRAPPING PAPER
SCISSORS

making a raffia bow
1. Take a handful of raffia from the bunch – about 20 strands – and cut both ends of the bundle level so all the strands are the same length. Remove 2 strands from the bunch and set aside. Make a loop at one end of the bunch, about 10 cm (4 inches) long.

2. Take the long end of the bunch back over the short end and form this in a loop to make a figure of eight.

3. Continue wrapping the long end around the figure of eight to form a thick bow.

4. Bind the centre of the bow tightly with the 2 reserved strands of raffia and tie them in a tight knot, leaving the ends long.

wrapping it up
5. Wrap the lily-of-the-valley crown in the wrapping paper, leaving the top open to show the flowers. Tie the raffia bow around the bundle using the loose ends to attach it.

hint
As they are living plants, keep the lily-of-the-valley roots moist right up until the last moment, then dab them dry before you wrap them, to prevent them wetting the paper. Encourage the recipient to place them in a cool position to enjoy the flowers, then plant them out in a moist, shady spot when the flowers have died down.

Gorgeous grape hyacinths

A collection of tiny glasses offers the perfect way to display a handful of grape hyacinths. The simple, but effective, arrangement reflects the beautiful delicacy of these tiny spring flowers. Arrange the glasses in a loose group or dotted about on a dining table, or enjoy them on your desk or window ledge.

Time to make: 15 minutes

what you need

3 SMALL BUNCHES OF GRAPE
   HYACINTHS (MUSCARI)
SMALL VASES OR GLASSES
SECATEURS

preparation

1. First fill a selection of small glasses or vases with water. Choose any number you like, the more the merrier. The glasses do not all have to be the same; a mixed collection can look just as effective. Add a little bleach to the water to keep it clear (see page 140).

cutting down to size

2. Using secateurs, trim the stems of the muscari to length. The length is critical, so measure the stems against the height of the glasses before you cut. Do this before splitting up the bunches, so they will all be the same length.

splitting up

3. Open up the bunches and select a few flowers and leaves for each glass. Vary the number of stems in each; some could have just one flower and others could have a small bunch of flowers and some leaves.

variation

Miniature daffodils (see right), with their cheerful faces and diminutive stature, will work just as well.

Jolly green giants

Tall green arums, paired with long stems of snake grass and wrapped in stripy calathea leaves, give an exotic feel to a simple, striking arrangement. The strong criss-cross lines and markings mean this sophisticated display works best against a light, unfussy background and acts as a stunning focal point to a room.

Time to make: 15 minutes

what you need
10 GREEN ARUMS
1 OR 2 CALATHEA LEAVES
BUNCH OF SNAKE GRASS
LARGE ROUND GLASS VASE
RAFFIA
SECATEURS
TOOTHPICK

making a start
1. Fill the vase about three-quarters full with water, to which a little bleach has been added (see page 140). Trim the arum stems to length and arrange them in the vase, interlocking the stems on the bottom of the vase so they support each other and you can position the central stems vertically.

positioning the leaf
2. Slide the leaf, stripy side out, into the vase and position it against the glass about a third of the way down. If the vase is very large or the leaves are small, you may need to use 2 leaves, one on either side of the vase, overlapping at both ends.

adding snake grass
3. Take a small bundle of snake grass stems, cut the ends level and bind them tightly together with raffia, about 8 cm (3 inches) from the base of the bundle. Twist the bundle so that the stems form a neat spiral at the bottom and a wide, open fan at the top. Place the fan of stems into the vase and lodge it among the arum stems so that it is supported in position with the bottoms of the stems under water.

hint
If you are using 2 calathea leaves, you can hold them in position by joining them together with a toothpick or small piece of stick. Use it like a stitch through both thicknesses of leaf.

Purple perfection

Deep purple anemones and maroon arums provide strong base notes for this rich, elegant arrangement; the ranunculus, bouvardia and viburnum provide a delicate lightness.

Time to make: 20 minutes

what you need
10 PALE PINK RANUNCULUS
10 MAROON ARUMS
LARGE BUNCH OF PURPLE
    ANEMONES
SMALL BUNCH OF GREEN
    BOUVARDIA
LARGE BUNCH OF WHITE
    VIBURNUM
SMALL GLASS VASE
SECATEURS

cutting down to size
1. Start by preparing all the flowers before you begin to arrange them. Trim all the stems to approximately the right length, then remove all the lower leaves. Make a pile of prepared stems of each variety. Take one stem from each pile to form a central core for the arrangement.

building up
2. Start to add more stems around the central core, adding each at an angle and working around the bunch to form a spiral effect (see page 140). This will create a full, domed effect with all the flowers facing outwards. Make sure that all of the different types of flowers are distributed evenly throughout the bunch. When the bunch is complete, cut all the stems level at the base.

final touches
3. Half-fill the vase with water to which a little bit of bleach has been added (see page 140). Place the flowers into the vase carefully to avoid upsetting the bunch. Assess the height of the flowers in relation to the vase and remove the bunch and trim the stems shorter if necessary.

hint
As the vase is quite small in relation to the number of flowers used, keep an eye on the water level and top up with a little bleach and water when necessary.

Easter nest

Perfect for an Easter gift, or a centrepiece for an Easter celebration, a simple bunch of sunny 'Yokohama' tulips grows out of a festive nest, with geese watching over their chocolate eggs on top. Great fun and delicious, too.

Time to make: 25 minutes

what you need
LARGE BUNCH OF TULIPS
TWIG BASKET
GLASS VASE OR JAR
RAFFIA
SCISSORS
SECATEURS
GOOSE DECORATIONS
CHOCOLATE EGGS
FEATHERS

the basic shape
1. Place the glass vase or jar into the basket and half-fill it with water. Take a bunch of raffia, about 30 strands, and cut both ends level. Wind the bunch around your hand to form a tight circle, then place it on top of the basket and tuck in the ends so the 'nest' stays in place.

making up the bunch
2. Strip all the lower leaves from the tulips to leave clean, bare stems. Gather the tulips, a few at a time, into a neat bunch in your hand, carefully positioning them so that the heads form a dense bunch.

taking shape
3. Tie the tulip stems together with raffia, tying it tight enough to hold the bunch, but avoid tying it so tight that the raffia cuts into the flower stems. Use secateurs to cut the stems level at the base and insert the stems into the vase or jar in the basket.

adding decorations
4. Decorate the basket with the geese decorations and chocolate eggs, balancing them on top of the raffia nest, then slip a few feathers among the strands of raffia.

Cool and elegant

Reminiscent of the Dutch Masters, this display uses parrot tulips and guelder rose in abundance, gracefully cascading over the edges of the glass tank. Tulips continue to grow after they have been cut; their stems lengthening and moving towards the light, so the display will evolve and change by the hour, making this a fascinating sight.

Time to make: 25 minutes

what you need
LARGE BUNCH OF GREEN
   PARROT TULIPS
LARGE BUNCH OF GUELDER
   ROSE (VIBURNUM OPULUS)
SQUARE GLASS VASE
RAFFIA
SECATEURS

tidying the stems
1. Strip the lower leaves from the stems of the tulips and guelder rose and remove any damaged or discoloured upper leaves.

building up
2. Take a few tulips and a few stems of guelder rose and form them into a bunch with all the heads level. Add a few more stems of each plant around the edges of the bunch, making sure the different flowers are evenly spread throughout the arrangement. You may find it easier to hold the bunch upside down as you add more stems because the flowers are quite floppy.

finishing the bunch
3. Turn the bunch up the right way at intervals to check the arrangement from the top. Form a large bundle of flowers with the outer flowers slightly lower than the central ones to form a dome shape (see page 140). Tie the stems together quite tightly with raffia, then trim off the stems level at the base. Half-fill the vase with water, to which a little bleach has been added (see page 140), then place the flowers into the vase.

hint
Don't worry if the tulips flop right down and hang over the edges of the vase; it is part of their charm.

Blue velvet

The vibrant blue of anemones and the silvery blue of thistles – sometimes called sea holly – make a perfect partnership in this modern and sleek design. The jagged, prickly leaves of the thistles contrast well with the velvety soft anemone petals.

Time to make: 25 minutes

what you need

LARGE BUNCH OF BLUE THISTLE
    (ERYNGIUM)
8–10 PURPLE ANEMONES
SQUARE GLASS VASE
RAFFIA
SMALL POT OR JAR
SECATEURS

preparing the thistles

1. Snip the heads off nearly all the blue thistle, reserving a few whole stems for the central bunch. Place the small pot or jar into the vase and fill with a little water. Arrange the thistle heads in the vase around the pot, filling the vase nearly to the rim. Take care to arrange some of the thistles facing outwards to show off their blue colour.

making up the posy

2. Arrange the remaining thistles and the purple anemones into a small, neat posy with the heads forming a rounded dome on top (see page 140).

final shaping

3. Tie the stems together with raffia, trim off the loose ends, then cut the stems level at the base. Place the stems inside the pot in the glass tank. Check the height of the posy and cut the stems again, if necessary.

hints

The thistle heads are quite hard and woody so they will not wilt without water. Do not compact the thistle heads too much in the vase or they will look squashed. Top up the little pot regularly with water as it is so small.

Protea paradise

This tropical burst of proteas and foliage will last for a long time – only the roses will really fade, so replace them with fresh flowers at intervals, leaving the permanent framework of proteas, bear grass and sword fern in position. The choice of pot is very important: its impact must be strong enough to balance the dense arrangement of flowers and leaves above.

Time to make: 25 minutes

what you need

7 WHITE PROTEAS
6 WHITE ROSES
14 SWORD FERN LEAVES
BUNCH OF BEAR GRASS
WHITE BOWL OR VASE
FLORIST'S FOAM
KNIFE
SECATEURS

starting out

1. Cut a piece of foam to fit the vase using a sharp knife (see page 136). Soak it in water until it is wet through, then place in the vase. Cut the fern fronds down to make shorter pieces, then remove the lower leaves to make a length of bare stem. Arrange 8 pieces of fern, equally spaced, around the edges of the vase to form a neat collar. Insert 1 protea stem vertically in the centre of the vase to set the maximum height.

taking shape

2. Add 3 shorter protea stems, equally spaced around the central flower. Insert them into the foam at an angle so that the flowers face outwards. Trim the thick white stems off the bunch of bear grass, then trim down the tips to make them all the same length, slightly longer than the central protea. Take 3 small bundles of bear grass from the bunch and insert them firmly into the foam between the proteas. Insert 3 ferns on the outside of the arranged bunches.

complete framework

3. Space 3 shorter proteas around the edges of the vase between the 3 medium ones. Add 3 shorter bunches of bear grass and 3 shorter ferns between them, in the same way as before. The long-lasting framework is now complete and there are 6 gaps to fill with temporary flowers, in this case the white roses.

adding the roses

4. Cut 3 roses to the height of the medium proteas and 3 to the height of the shortest ones. Insert the roses into the gaps in between the proteas, according to height.

variations

Proteas are also available in red and pink, though they look much softer and prettier in white. You could do this display with red or pink proteas with matching roses, or you could replace white roses with ones of a different colour when the white ones fade. Try soft orange or a creamy yellow for a much warmer effect.

Spring greens

Here, celestial orchids are planted into a mundane wash bin to provide a piece of heaven on earth. The combination of twisted willow twigs and soft moss creates a good mix of textures and shapes. This version is party-sized, and could be scaled down for a more intimate setting.

Time to make: 30 minutes

what you need
LARGE GALVANISED CONTAINER
POLYSTYRENE CHUNKS
ORCHID COMPOST
3 POTTED CYMBIDIUM ORCHIDS
TWISTED WILLOW TWIGS
BUN MOSS

ensuring drainage

1. Half-fill the container with large chunks of either polystyrene or other light-weight drainage material, then add a deep layer of compost, filling the container to within 15 cm (6 inches) of the rim. Remove the orchids from their pots and plant in the compost, firming it back around their roots.

filling the pot

2. Add more compost if necessary to fill any gaps or level the surface. Insert a few twisted willow stems into the compost between the orchids.

covering the compost

3. Water the compost very thoroughly, then cover the surface with bun moss, pushing the pieces close together so that there are no gaps.

variation

Cymbidiums are among the easiest of orchids to look after, but many other types could be used in this display. Check their growing requirements first as some are more easy to accommodate than others.

hints

Place the orchids in a bright position with plenty of diffused light, not direct sunlight. Keep the compost just moist, but water more frequently in early spring to encourage flowering. Remember to feed the plants around this time, too.

Mother's day bouquet

A Mother's day surprise in glorious spring colours – acid green euphorbia, soft blue hyacinths and primrose-yellow tulips. All beautifully wrapped and with a fragrance to fill the house, this is the perfect gift to show you care. Be sure to mention you made it yourself.

Time to make: 30 minutes

what you need

BUNCH OF YELLOW TULIPS
LARGE BUNCH OF BLUE
   HYACINTHS
SALAL LEAVES
EUPHORBIA
RAFFIA
SECATEURS
WRAPPING PAPER

starting the posy
1. Prepare all the flowers and foliage by removing the lower leaves to leave clean, bare stems. Make a central core by selecting a few stems of each type and forming them into a neat posy.

building up
2. Add further stems around the outside of the central core, alternating between the different flowers and foliage to achieve an even balance (see page 140). Keep viewing the bunch from different angles as you make it to make sure the effect is full from all sides. Add the tulips in pairs to add more impact. Finish with a number of salal stems around the outside.

trimming to size
3. When you have used up all the flowers and are happy with the bouquet, trim the ends of the stems to the same length as the hyacinth stems. Avoid cutting the hyacinth stems themselves.

final touches
4. Tie the stems securely with raffia in a neat knot and trim off the loose ends.

5. Wrap the bouquet in paper and finish with a raffia bow.

warning
Euphorbia sap can be an irritant, so wear gloves if you have sensitive skin.

summer

Cosmos (*Cosmos*) These striking, daisy-like single flowers are available throughout the summer and into autumn in shades of white and pink. Their simple form will grace many summer arrangements.

Stocks (*Matthiola*) Densely-packed white, pink or mauve spikes of stocks are good for adding vertical emphasis to arrangements. The sweet, peppery scent epitomizes summer.

Peonies (*Paeonia*) These massive, showy flowers look fantastic in a mixed bunch or placed singly in a simple arrangement. They flower in early summer and are available in shades of white, pink, red, crimson and maroon. Many have a delicious sweet fragrance.

Roses (*Rosa*) Available in almost every shade of red, pink, white, yellow and orange, as well as more unusual colours, roses are versatile and beautiful in any arrangement. Though they are around all year, they will always be reminiscent of summer gardens.

Lilies (*Lilium*) These striking flowers come in many sizes and in colours ranging from the purest white to the bright orange of the tiger lily. They last well when cut, but beware of pollen stains on clothes and furniture (see page 140).

Cornflowers (*Centaurea cyanus*) Although they are now also available in pink or white, it is the vivid blue cornflowers found in traditional cornfields, that are the most beautiful and the most useful in flower arranging due to their striking colour.

Champagne cocktail

A sweet, fizzy concoction in pastel pink and white, with bubbles leaping out of the glass. This is not, in fact, an arrangement of small flowers, but just one allium head with a few sweet peas added around the edge of the glass. Perfect to serve at drinks parties!

Time to make: 10 minutes

what you need
DRINKS MEASURE
COCKTAIL GLASS
1 ALLIUM HEAD
PINK AND WHITE SWEET PEAS
COCKTAIL PARASOL
SECATEURS

mix the drink...
1. Pour 2 measures of water into the cocktail glass. Cut the stem off the allium, leaving just a short stump and place the head in the glass so the stump is well submerged under the water.

...add a garnish
2. Trim the sweet peas into small pieces, leaving each piece with a few flowers and a short length of stem.

...and serve!
3. Arrange the sweet peas around the allium head, mixing the colours. Decorate with the parasol and serve!

Flowers in space

The striking heads of scabious and curcuma emerging from a metallic vase make a futuristic, space-age arrangement that looks stunning in a modern, minimalist room.

Time to make: 15 minutes

what you need

6 CURCUMA STEMS
10 SCABIOUS SEEDHEADS
TALL METALLIC VASE
FLORIST'S FOAM
KNIFE
SECATEURS

the basic shape

1. Cut the foam to fit the vase (see page 136), then soak it in water until it is wet through. Push the soaked foam into the vase, making sure that it reaches the base. Cut 5 curcuma stems to the same length and insert in a circular pattern in the foam.

the inner circle

2. Cut 5 scabious stems to an even length slightly longer than the curcuma stems and use them to make a circle inside the curcumas.

the outer circle

3. Cut the remaining 5 scabious to a much shorter length and insert into the foam around the edges of the vase, equally spaced as before.

the final touch

4. Insert the remaining curcuma stem in the centre of the arrangement.

hint

Cut the thick curcuma stems at an angle to make them easier to insert into the foam.

Summer cornfield

This natural arrangement was inspired by a cornfield in the height of summer, with a tangle of wild flowers among the straight shafts of corn. Arrange the flowers in random clumps within the display, to create the effect of a bunch picked straight from the edge of a field.

Time to make: 15 minutes

what you need

LARGE BUNCH OF CORNFLOWERS
LARGE BUNCH OF FRESH WHEAT
LARGE BUNCH OF ALCHEMILLA
LARGE BUNCH OF NIGELLA
CYLINDRICAL GLASS VASE
SECATEURS

preparation

1. Prepare the stems of all the flowers and the wheat by stripping off the lower leaves. Arrange the different flowers in neat piles to make arranging easier. Start with a central bunch, made up of a few stems of each of the different flowers and foliage.

making up the bunch

2. Add flowers around the outside of the central bunch at an angle to form a slight spiral (see page 140). Add a few stems of each of the different varieties at one time for added impact.

Arrange the flowers so that the heads form a soft dome shape, with the heads of wheat occasionally breaking out of the dome. Add the remaining flowers lower down around the sides of the arrangement. Cut all the stems level at the bottom and place in the vase.

variation

Substitute the cornflowers with single red poppies or frothy white dill to keep the wild flower look.

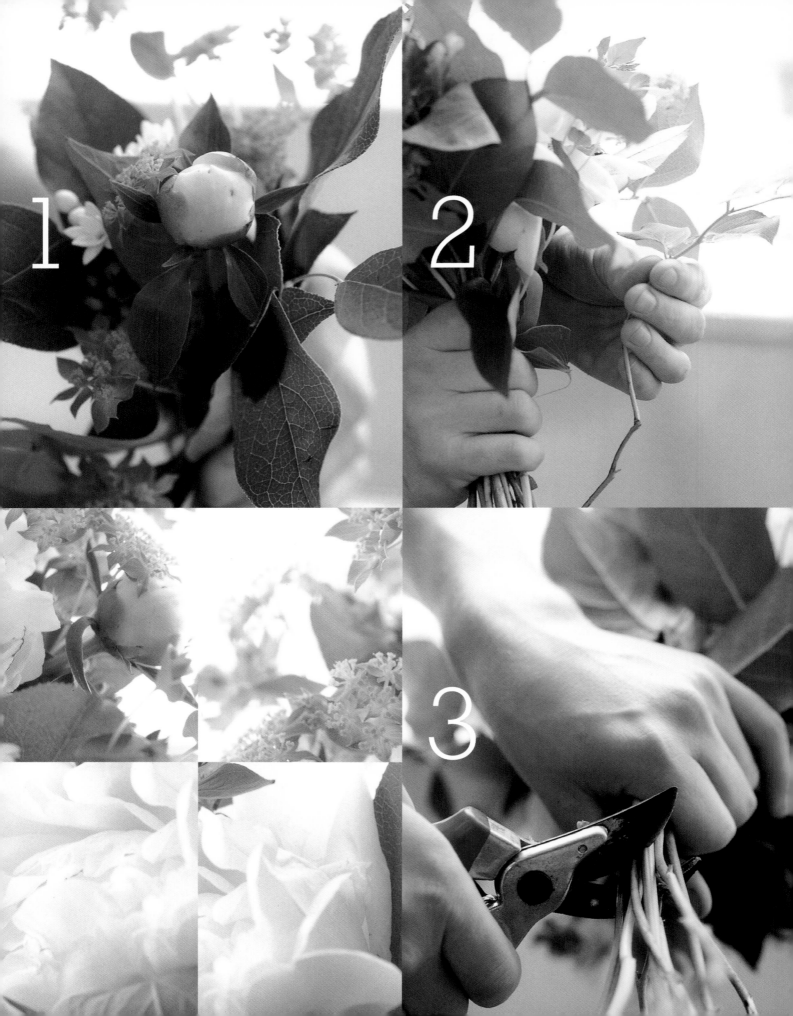

Afternoon tea

Pairing two traditional silver rose vases creates a really smart look, making this arrangement perfect for either an afternoon tea table or a modern table setting. The white peonies look stunning set off against the dark green foliage and smaller flowers. The scent of the peonies is simply amazing.

Time to make: 20 minutes

what you need

SALAL FOLIAGE

6–10 PEONY STEMS

SMALL BUNCH OF WHITE
   BOUVARDIA

SMALL BUNCH OF BUPLEURUM

2 SILVER VASES

SECATEURS

preparations

1. Strip the lower leaves from the salal and the bouvardia to leave bare stems. Start by making a small central bunch, with a peony bud in the middle and a stem or so of the other materials around the outside.

making up the bunch

2. Add further stems around the outside of the central bunch at a slight angle to form a loose spiral (see page 140). Make sure the different flowers and foliage are evenly spread throughout the bunch. Aim to form a domed posy with the peonies recessed slightly amongst the other material.

filling the vases

3. Cut the stems level at the base of the bunch and place carefully in the vase, so as not to upset the bunch. Repeat to fill the second vase. Top the vases up with some water.

variation

Deep red peonies would make a much more exotic display, suitable for an evening occasion.

Think pink

Peonies are eternal favourites because they are such luxurious flowers. They can be dressed up or dressed down to suit your mood. In this relaxed, bold display, the flowers are arranged in small groups of the same variety so that the display looks natural and not overly styled.

Time to make: 25 minutes

what you need
5 PINK PEONIES
5 PURPLE ALLIUMS
BUNCH OF PINK AND PURPLE
    STOCKS
MAGNOLIA FOLIAGE
ZEUS BERRY
GALVANISED JUG
SECATEURS
ELASTIC BAND

initial steps
1. Strip the leaves from the lower stems of all the flowers and foliage. Take 3 stems of the Zeus berry and add 3 stems of each of the other materials to form a bunch.

forming a bunch
2. Add further stems around the central bunch at a slight angle to form a spiral, keeping each element grouped together (see page 140). Aim to form a dome with the heads, allowing the stocks and Zeus berries to be slightly taller.

taking shape
3. When all the flowers are used up, add a few more stems of magnolia leaf around the outside, then secure the stems with an elastic band (see page 139).

stem support
4. Cut the stems level at the base, then place into the jug. Check the height of the flowers and foliage; the lowest leaves should be resting lightly on the jug rim. If the stems are too long, cut them a bit shorter. Top the jug up with water.

variation
The stocks could be replaced with some pink or burgundy antirrhinums. Add frothy white dill for a softer look.

Scented, shiny and sophisticated

Sophisticated 'Pompeii' lilies and creamy white roses displayed in a funky blue bowl are made even more stunning by using the darkest and shiniest magnolia leaves that can be found. The rusty-brown, velvety undersides of the leaves add a further contrast of colour and textures and the heavy scent of the lilies is fantastic.

Time to make: 25 minutes

what you need
4 STEMS OF 'POMPEII' LILIES
10 WHITE ROSES
MAGNOLIA FOLIAGE
GLASS BOWL
SECATEURS

preparing the stems
1. Strip the leaves off the lower stems of the lilies, magnolia and roses and remove the rose thorns. Half-fill the vase with water and arrange 3 lily stems in the vase, equally spaced around the rim, with the stems crossing in the middle.

the basic frame
2. Arrange 3 stems of magnolia between the lilies in a symmetrical pattern, locking the stems in place between the lily stems to form a criss-cross framework.

adding the roses
3. Trim the rose stems down to length and arrange 6 stems, equally spaced, around the inside edge of the vase, wriggling the stems down between the other stems to hold them in place.

the high point
4. Insert the remaining stem of lilies right into the top of the display, again wriggling the stem into position.

filling gaps
5. Finish the display by adding a few extra roses and foliage stems to fill gaps and add highlights. Try to add each rose where it will be framed by foliage.

hints
Remove the stamens from the lilies to stop the pollen staining furniture and clothes (see page 140). Choose a bowl with a narrow neck as it will help to support the flowers in position. It is easiest to start with large sprays of flowers and foliage to get the balance right, then move on to smaller flowers and pieces of foliage to fill in the gaps.

Hydrangea topiary

This stylish arrangement is great for table decorations, even weddings. The simple shape is formed by one perfect hydrangea head, into which are woven velvety red roses and spiky blue thistles. Its mixture of textures and colours is best appreciated close-up.

Time to make: 25 minutes

what you need

1 HYDRANGEA HEAD
10 RED ROSES
SMALL BUNCH OF BLUE THISTLES
 (ERYNGIUM)
10–12 HOSTA LEAVES
GLASS BOWL
RAFFIA
SECATEURS

preparing the stems

1. Prepare the hydrangea head by stripping off all the leaves from the stem. Trim the blue thistle stems and strip the leaves and thorns off all of the rose stems.

inserting the flowers

2. Hold the hydrangea by the stem and carefully insert the rose and eryngium stems between the florets. Aim to space them evenly through the hydrangea head, making sure they follow the shape of the hydrangea, rather than break the surface.

making the collar

3. When all the flowers are in place, arrange the hosta leaves around the outside to form a collar. Tie the stems securely together, then cut off the bottoms to make them level, leaving them quite short. Half-fill the bowl with water, then place the stems in it. The hosta leaves should sit on the rim of the bowl, so adjust the length of the stems if necessary.

Wild hedgerow

This soft, informal combination of pinks, whites and lilac stirs up an image of countryside hedgerows, with oak leaves, roses and wild flowers in abundance. The arrangement is also shaped like a hedge, thick and densely packed at the base and tapering out towards the top.

Time to make: 30 minutes

what you need

SMALL BUNCH OF SPEARMINT

7 LILAC ROSES

FEW BRODIAEA STEMS

FEW WHITE PENSTEMON STEMS
  (PENSTEMON 'SNOWSTORM')

SMALL BUNCH OF WHITE
  LYSIMACHIA

OAK FOLIAGE

CRACKLE-GLAZED POT

FLORIST'S FOAM

KNIFE

SECATEURS

the basic framework

1. Cut a piece of foam to fit the pot using a sharp knife (see page 136). Soak it in water until it is wet through, then push it into the pot. It should be a tight fit. Prepare the flower stems by stripping off the lower leaves. Start by inserting a few small sprigs of oak around the edges of the pot to form a circle, then insert one penstemon stem in the centre of the pot to set the maximum height.

around the edges

2. Add a stem each of rose, lysimachia and spearmint close to the central stem, but with the heads lower down.

taking shape

3. Add a group of 3 brodiaea stems together. Add more flowers and foliage to the arrangement, aiming for an even distribution and creating an even profile from the tallest stem in the centre to the rim of oak leaves.

filling in

4. Continue adding the brodiaea in groups of three. Turn the pot regularly to fill in any gaps and to create a natural, full arrangement.

hints

Always start with plenty of foliage and then add the flowers so you will achieve an even and natural balance of foliage and flowers. Wet the foam regularly with water as there are so many flowers in this arrangement.

Gloriously fruitful

This colourful table centrepiece is a luxurious feast for the eyes, a warm mix of rich reds and mauves, made more vibrant by the addition of acid green. The cherries and redcurrants in the display make it perfect for a wedding celebration, as fruit symbolises fertility in many cultures. It looks good enough to eat!

Time to make: 25 minutes

what you need
SMALL BUNCH OF ALCHEMILLA
20 DEEP PURPLE SWEET PEAS
5 GLORIOSA STEMS
BAG OF CHERRIES
½ PUNNET OF REDCURRANTS
FLAT GLASS BOWL
SCISSORS

decorating the rim
1. Start by filling the dish with water. Trim the alchemilla into small sprigs and arrange some around the rim of the dish with their stems in the water.

edging the dish
2. Trim sprigs of foliage from the gloriosa stems and arrange it in the centre of the dish. Trim the sweet pea stems short and insert them amongst the alchemilla around the edges of the dish.

adding the heads
3. Arrange a few of the gloriosa flower heads among the other flowers, making sure their stems are under the water.

the central mound
4. Arrange a large double handful of cherries in the centre of the bowl among the flowers.

topping up
5. Place a few more sweet pea and gloriosa flowers and a few sprigs of gloriosa foliage on top of the cherries, wriggling their stems into the water below.

filling in the gaps
6. Add a few more cherries to fill any gaps, then arrange some redcurrant sprigs on the rim of the bowl, draped on top of the foliage and flowers and hanging over the edge.

variation
Use limes or blueberries instead of cherries.

hint
To maximize its lifespan, place the bowl in a cool place out of direct sunlight and top up the water regularly. This arrangement will last for about a week.

Summer meadow

This natural arrangement encapsulates the feel of a lush wildflower meadow on a warm summer's day. Place in a cool, bright room or on the doorstep to bring a slice of the countryside to your home.

Time to make: 40 minutes

what you need

3 ICELAND POPPIES IN POTS
6 ORNAMENTAL GRASSES IN POTS
3 WHITE COSMOS IN POTS
LARGE GALVANISED CONTAINER
POTTING COMPOST
TROWEL
DRAINAGE MATERIAL (OPTIONAL)

filling the container

1. Fill the container with compost to within 10 cm (4 inches) of the rim. If there are no drainage holes in the container, either make some first, or add a layer of drainage material before adding the compost (see page 142). A deep layer of pebbles, chunks of broken polystyrene or gravel would be suitable.

planning

2. Plan the arrangement before removing any of the plants from their pots, by placing them on top of the compost and moving them around until they look right.

removing the pots

3. When you have planned their positions, remove the plants from their pots and tease out a few of the roots if they are tightly bound.

planting

4. Ease the rootballs into the compost in the container so that the tops are just below the rim of the pot.

filling in

5. Add a little more compost to fill any gaps between the plants and level the surface, if necessary.

6. Firm the compost gently around the plants' roots, adding more compost to fill if needed. Water well to moisten the compost.

hints

Water the plants an hour before planting in the container to make sure the compost surrounding their roots is wet.

Use a free-draining potting compost in the container. Keep the compost just moist at all times, and remember to water regularly during hot weather.

Feed the container with a liquid fertilizer during the spring and summer.

Bacchanal urn

A classical metal urn filled with luxurious flowers in rich blues and greens and soft pale pink. The grapes enhance the bacchanal feel of this sumptuous erotic creation. For maximum impact, place against a mirror, preferably one with a heavy gilt frame.

Time to make: 45 minutes

what you need
4 DARK BLUE DELPHINIUMS
5 BELLS OF IRELAND
   (MOLUCELLA)
5 PALE BLUE AGAPANTHUS
8 PINK ROSES
BUNCH OF EUPHORBIA
2 BUNCHES OF BLACK GRAPES
URN OR LARGE POT
FLORIST'S FOAM
KNIFE
SECATEURS
CELLOPHANE
SCISSORS

preparing the urn

1. Line the urn with cellophane to protect the inside (see page 136). Cut a piece of foam to fit the urn snugly using a sharp knife. Soak the foam in water until it is wet right through, then push it into the urn. Cut off the excess cellophane.

the basic frame

2. Strip the lower leaves off the delphinium stems. Place one tall stem at the back of the arrangement in the centre, then 2 stems slightly further forward at the sides and a much shorter stem at the front.

extending the fan

3. Strip the lower leaves off the bells of Ireland and insert 2 stems at the back of the arrangement either side of the central delphinium. Angle the stems so that they are leaning outwards to form a fan shape. Insert one stem of bells of Ireland in the middle of the arrangement between the 2 medium height delphiniums, and 2 shorter stems either side of the shortest delphinium, again aiming to retain the fan shape.

filling in

4. Arrange the agapanthus stems evenly throughout the arrangement at different heights, within the overall fan shape to fill it out. Now add the roses within the framework, spacing them evenly as highlights and to fill any gaps.

final touches

5. Use the euphorbia to bulk out the arrangement where it looks a bit thin, especially around the bottom. Insert the stems between the other flowers, recessing some deep within the framework. Snip the bunches of grapes in several smaller pieces. Cut some discarded rose stems into short lengths and use them to anchor the grapes into the foam. Arrange the grapes around the rim of the urn.

autumn

▼ Apples
Apples and other autumn fruits and vegetables make attractive and varied additions to harvest or Hallowe'en displays. There are so many varieties, it is easy to find the right colour and shape for your arrangement.

▼ Mophead chrysanthemums
Not simply for flower shows, these large flowers are grown in all shades of pink, yellow, red, orange and white, many with more than one colour on the flower. Choose the oranges, yellows and golds for autumn arrangements. Great for big, bold splashes of colour.

▲ Roses (*Rosa*)
Use the orange, red, russet and gold varieties in displays for a vibrant and warm seasonal effect at this time of year. Avoid those that are tightly budded as they may not open right out.

▼ Slipper orchids (*Paphiopedilum*)
The large, shiny flowers are born on long stalks and add a truly exotic note to an autumn arrangement. Many come in russet tones, often with rich green and purple spots on the flowers, too. The long-lasting blooms can be used as cut flowers, or buy potted plants to enjoy next year as well.

▼ Arum (*Zantedeschia*)
A truly sculptural flower that looks stunning whatever you do with it, whether massed in a simple vase or used sparingly among other 'filler' flowers. The wonderful orange varieties are perfect for autumn, but look out for rich pinks, soft lemons and deep maroons and purples.

▲ Hydrangea (*Hydrangea*)
These beautiful large flowerheads are spectacular in simple arrangements or can be used to add background texture for feature flowers in mixed displays. They come in rich red, deep maroon, bright pink, clear blue and white. Hydrangeas slowly dry in an arrangement and can be used in dried displays afterwards. They retain their colour well.

Autumn sunshine

As the summer comes to an end and the days begin to get shorter, the bright yellow of sunflowers serves to cheer us up and prolong the feeling of sunshine. The chequerboard patterns of the dried corn cobs echo the pattern in the heart of the sunflower. The filled galvanized buckets are sufficiently heavy to stop the flowers tipping over.

Time to make: 15 minutes

what you need
3 SUNFLOWERS
9 DRIED MINI CORN COBS
3 SMALL GALVANIZED BUCKETS
FLORIST'S FOAM
KNIFE
CELLOPHANE
SCISSORS

lining the buckets

1. Line the buckets with cellophane to make them watertight. Cut the foam, with a sharp knife, to fit the base of the buckets. Soak the foam in water until it is wet through and place in the buckets. The top of the foam should be about 2.5 cm (1 inch) below the rim of the buckets. Cut off the excess cellophane with scissors.

cutting to size

2. Cut the sunflowers to the same length. Think carefully before you cut, as the height is quite critical to balance the display. Insert 1 stem into the foam in the centre of each bucket.

adding the cobs

3. Arrange 3 corn cobs on top of the foam around each sunflower stem. Arrange all 3 facing the same way in each pot. Tuck in the leaves to neaten the appearance.

hint

Sunflowers are thirsty flowers, so top the buckets up regularly with water to keep the foam moist.

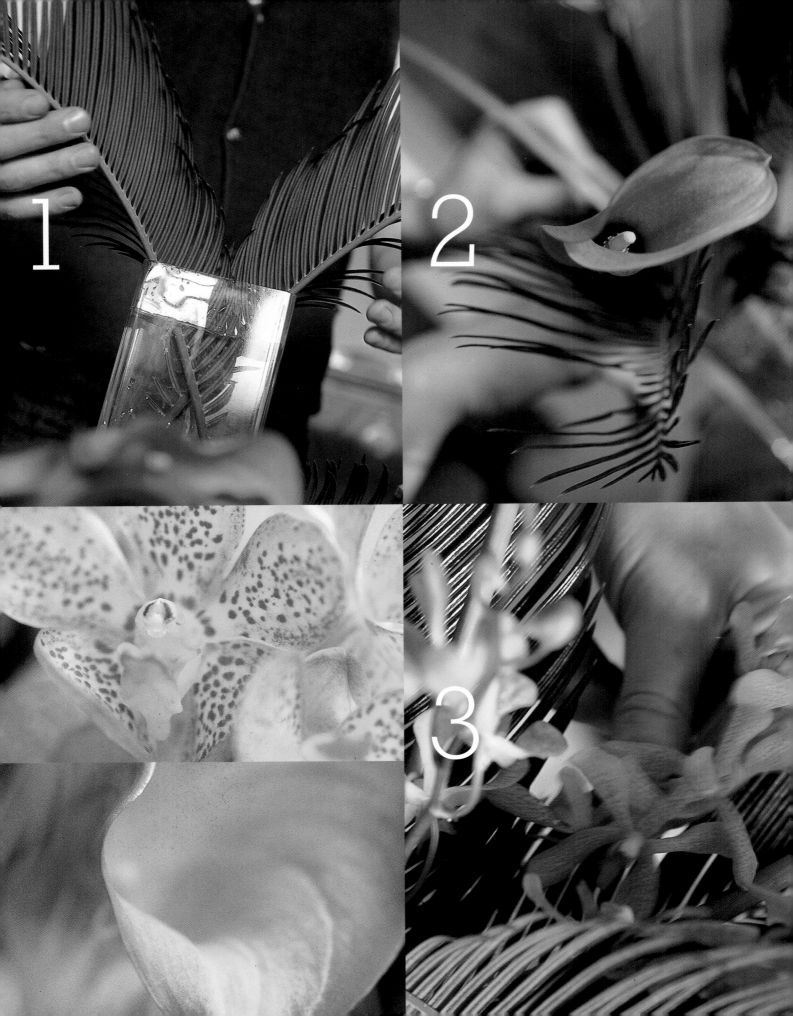

Exotic sculpture

Rich orange arums and spotty spray orchids are available all year, but their deep tones make them perfect for autumn. Here they are arranged with sculptural cycas leaves. Despite the exotic nature of the flowers and leaves, this is in fact a very simple arrangement, set off beautifully by a clear glass vase.

Time to make: 15 minutes

what you need

3 ORANGE ARUMS
3 CYCAS LEAVES
SMALL BUNCH OF ORANGE
    SPRAY ORCHIDS
SQUARE GLASS VASE
SECATEURS

perfect symmetry
1. Fill the vase about three-quarters full with water, to which a little bleach has been added (see page 140). Arrange the cycas leaves evenly in the vase, 1 on each side and 1 in the middle. Try to use the natural curve of the leaves to position them where they look best. Interlock the stems in the vase so that they support each other.

the central core
2. Arrange the arums in the centre of the arrangement, inserting the stems between the cycas stems to hold them in place.

filling the gaps
3. Add a few sprays of orchids low down to fill gaps and add bulk to the display. Again, insert the stems between the others to form a rigid framework.

Carnation creation

Despite their commonplace reputation, carnations still have something to offer the flower connoisseur, as this simple but stylish idea proves. They are easy to find, they last forever and these clashing colours are perfect for this time of year. Be bold!

Time of project: 15 minutes

what you need

5 ORANGE CARNATIONS
5 RED CARNATIONS
5 PINK CARNATIONS
ALUMINIUM POT
SECATEURS
GRAVEL
FLORIST'S TAPE

making the dome

1. Start with 1 carnation of each colour. Hold the stems close to the heads and arrange the flowers so that they form a flat surface on top. Continue to add flowers to the bunch, 1 at a time, alternating the colours. Aim to make a rounded mushroom shape with the flower heads, arranging them close together with their top surfaces aligned.

taping the stems

2. When the dome is complete, tape the stems tightly together about 8 cm (3 inches) from the heads using florist's tape. Tape the stems again about 8 cm (3 inches) from the base and trim them to an even length.

standing firm

3. Place the stems into the pot and hold them right in the centre. Pour gravel around them to fill the pot to the rim. Top the pot up with water.

variation

This arrangement could also be made with peonies or roses in the summer on a larger scale.

Prickly perfection

This autumnal group, in a classic bouquet shape, has a beautiful mixture of tones and textures. The deep red roses are offset by the pale blue tones of the thistles, a contrast echoed by the dark purple smoke bush foliage and the light green bouvardia.

Time to make: 25 minutes

what you need

12 RED ROSES

LARGE BUNCH OF BLUE THISTLE (ERYNGIUM)

LARGE BUNCH OF GREEN BOUVARDIA

PURPLE SMOKE BUSH FOLIAGE (COTINUS)

CHRISTMAS BOX WITH BERRIES (SARCOCOCCA)

SMALL GLASS VASE

SECATEURS

the central core

1. Fill the vase about three-quarters full with water, to which a little bleach has been added (see page 140). Strip the lower leaves off the stems of all the flowers and foliage before you begin. Start the arrangement with a small central core of flowers: 1 rose, 1 stem of blue thistle and 1 stem of bouvardia. Arrange them into a tight, neat bunch.

the inner ring

2. Next add a ring of about 3 stems of Christmas box around the flowers. Position the stems at a slight angle to the central bunch to make a spiral around the outside (see page 140).

the outer ring

3. Continue to add stems around the outside of the bunch, mixing the different flowers and foliage evenly. Maintain the spiral, adding the stems at a slight angle and working around the bunch in the same direction. When the bunch is complete, cut the stems straight across the bottom.

checking the fit

4. Position the bunch in the vase and check the height; the lower leaves should sit on the vase rim. If it is necessary, remove the bunch and retrim the stems, taking care not to upset the bunch as you do so.

Urban jungle

Use elegant white gladioli to create this cool, calm, ultra-modern display. The impact of white flowers against the green leaves is heightened by the use of strong, broad cheese plant leaves with tall, spiky gladioli.

Time to make: 25 minutes

what you need

4 CHEESE PLANT LEAVES
    (MONSTERA)
LARGE BUNCH OF WHITE
    GLADIOLI
4 GREEN ANTHURIUMS
BUNCH OF EUCALYPTUS FOLIAGE
LARGE GLASS VASE
SECATEURS

hiding the rim

1. Fill the vase with water, to which a little bleach has been added (see page 140). Start by positioning the cheese plant leaves evenly around the rim of the vase, interlocking the stems in the bottom of the vase to hold them in place.

adding height

2. Next add the gladioli, trimming the stems to a similar height to make a circle of stems in the vase. Leave 2 of the stems taller and arrange these in the centre of the display. Insert the stems between the interlocked cheese plant stems to hold them in place.

adding depth

3. Next add the anthuriums low down in the arrangement with their stamens pointing downwards gracefully.

filling the gaps

4. Finish off by adding stems of eucalyptus foliage to fill gaps and add colour on all sides of the arrangement.

hint

Remove the topmost bud of the gladioli spires. This is said to encourage the lower buds to open more quickly.

Maroon on black

A velvety display of the darkest red dahlias and blood-red leucodendron foliage, with contrasting green bouvardia, in a black shiny bowl; a sumptuous and dramatic mingling of textures and tones. A collar of galax leaves sits prettily around the rim of the bowl, heightening the impact.

Time to make: 25 minutes

what you need

LARGE BUNCH OF RED DAHLIAS

5 STEMS OF GREEN BOUVARDIA

LEUCODENDRON 'SAFARI GOLD' FOLIAGE

FLAT ROUND LEAVES, SUCH AS GALAX OR IVY

BLACK BOWL

SECATEURS

central core

1. Fill the vase with water. Strip the lower leaves off the leucodendron, dahlia and bouvardia stems. Start by making a small bunch for the central core. Arrange a single piece of bouvardia in the centre with 3 stems of leucodendron around the outside (see page 140). Arrange 3 dahlia stems between the leucodendron stems in order to keep the arrangement symmetrical.

making the dome

2. Add 3 more stems of bouvardia, evenly spaced around the outside, then add dahlias and leucodendron alternately around the edges to increase the bunch. The stems should just cross at the bottom so that the flower heads can form a neat dome on top.

trimming to size

3. Keep checking the arrangement from all sides as you position the flowers. When all of the flowers have been used, cut the stems level at the base, holding the flowers tightly in place.

making the collar

4. Place the bunch in the vase. Trim down the stems of the galax or ivy leaves and make a neat collar of leaves around the edges of the vase.

Classical chic

What could have been a stuffy, formal arrangement has become a chic and pretty party piece by pairing the over-the-top forms and colours of poppy seedheads, lime green chrysanthemums and shocking pink dahlias with a classical gold urn.

Time to make: 30 minutes

what you need
10–12 'SHAMROCK'
    CHRYSANTHEMUMS
10–12 PINK DAHLIAS
10–12 POPPY SEEDHEADS
SMALL URN
FLORIST'S FOAM
KNIFE
CELLOPHANE
SCISSORS
SECATEURS

preparing the urn

1. Line the urn with a sheet of cellophane to make it watertight (see page 136). Cut a piece of florist's foam with a sharp knife, so it fits the base of the urn, then soak it in water until it is wet through; position in the urn. Let the foam protrude above the rim of the urn to give you more surface to insert the flower stems. Cut off the excess cellophane. Insert a poppy head in the centre and then add 2 chrysanthemums and 2 dahlias alternately around it. Cross the stems in the foam at the base so the flowers face outwards.

building up the globe

2. Arrange 4 more poppy seedheads around the outside of the arrangement between the flowers, keeping the display symmetrical.

full circle

3. Arrange 2 more of the chrysanthemums, to either side and below each of the dahlias to form a triangle, and then add 2 dahlias to either side and below each original chrysanthemum. Then add a row of poppies around the bottom and tuck in extra flowers around the base to fill any gaps right down to the pot rim, still keeping the arrangement as symmetrical as possible.

hint

Try to get the positioning right the first time. As there are so many flower stems in a small piece of foam, the foam will break up quickly if you have to keep removing and repositioning stems.

Russet autumn basket

The rich, russet tones and heavy foliage set into a stout basket make this a classic autumn arrangement, but the sumptuous 'Leonidas' roses and mottled brassica heads give it an elegant twist. Perfect for a candle-lit meal, or just enjoying around the home.

Time to make: 40 minutes

what you need

3 RED HYDRANGEA HEADS
3–4 BRASSICA HEADS
6–8 'LEONIDAS' ROSES
SMALL BUNCH OF HYPERICUM
    BERRIES
RHODODENDRON FOLIAGE
BASKET
FLORIST'S FOAM
KNIFE
CELLOPHANE
SCISSORS
SECATEURS

preparation

1. Line the basket with cellophane to make it watertight (see page 136). Cut a piece of foam to fit the inside of the basket, soak it in water until it is wet through, then position in the basket. Trim off the excess cellophane. Cut the rhododendron foliage into short sprigs, each with a length of stem, then start to insert pieces of the foliage into the foam around the edges of the basket.

making the dome

2. Continue to add the rhododendron foliage until you have built up a neat dome of foliage inside the basket, right down to the edges on all sides.

creating form

3. Cut the hydrangea stems to fit the size of the basket and insert them into the foam between the foliage, equally spaced in the basket.

4. Trim down the brassica stems at an angle to make them easier to insert into the foam. Space the heads evenly in the basket.

adding the roses

5. Strip the leaves and thorns off the rose stems and trim them to size. Position the roses evenly in the display, leaving them protruding slightly above the foliage.

filling gaps

6. Strip the lower leaves off the hypericum stems, trim the stems to size and add to the arrangement, using them to fill any gaps and add textural interest.

variation

Add a few white flowers to the display if you want it to be brighter. White or cream roses would go well.

hints

Pour a cup of water over the foam every other day to keep it moist.
The hydrangeas will gradually dry in the arrangement and can be used in another display afterwards. They keep their colour well.

Bizarre beauty

The impact of this long-lasting, growing arrangement lies in the contrast of shapes and textures between the upright ivy, exotic orchids and the bizarre, ground-hugging bead plants. This is an ideal display for any living room – traditional or modern.

Time to make: 40 minutes

what you need
2 SLIPPER ORCHIDS IN POTS
   (PAPHIOPEDILUM)
6–8 BEAD PLANTS (NERTERA)
1 POT OF UPRIGHT IVY (HEDERA
   HELIX 'CONGESTA')
BASKET
CELLOPHANE
SCISSORS
PEBBLES
HOUSEPLANT COMPOST
MOSS

preparing the basket
1. Line the basket with cellophane to make it fully watertight (see page 136), then arrange a layer of pebbles in the bottom as drainage material.

arranging the orchids
2. Place a layer of compost in the bottom of the basket, then stand the orchids, still in their pots, on top, arranging them side by side. The tops of the pots should lie just below the level of the rim of the basket.

adding the ivy
3. Add more compost around the orchids' pots and firm. Remove the ivy from its pot and plant it between and just behind the orchids. Firm the roots into the compost and add more around them to bring the level up to 5 cm (2 inches) below the rim of the basket.

covering the ground
4. Remove the bead plants from their pots and plant in the compost around the orchids, positioning them close together so that they cover the compost with their foliage and berries.

filling the gaps
5. Fill any gaps between the bead plants with moss to cover the compost entirely, particularly around the orchids' pots. Trim off the excess cellophane around the edge of the basket and tuck in the edges. Water well to moisten the compost and feed the orchids and bead plants regularly to maintain healthy growth.

hint
Leave the orchids in their pots as they will be growing in special orchid compost.

Hallowe'en candelabra

This baroque candelabra is superb as a scene-stealing centrepiece for a Hallowe'en party. It can be made on a much smaller scale, however, using a small candelabra, when it would be great for a Hallowe'en dinner party, with fruits and nuts piled round it on the table. Leave out the pumpkins if space is limited.

Time to make: 45 minutes

what you need
METAL CANDELABRA
CANDLES
IVY TRAILS
POMEGRANATES
PUMPKINS
APPLES
CHESTNUTS
SECATEURS

covering the metal
1. Select several trails of ivy at a time and hold them together in a bunch. Wind the bunch around an arm of the candelabra until the ends are quite short, then tuck them in. Continue to wind bunches of ivy trails around the candelabra, criss-crossing them in different directions to cover the metal completely.

loose ends
2. Leave the ends of the ivy trails loose at the ends of the candelabra arms, allowing them to fan out in an attractive spray.

attaching the fruit
3. This candelabra has spikes on the arms, so I have speared pomegranates onto them. They could, however, be wired into place (see page 139).

covering the base
4. When the candelabra is completely covered with ivy, pile the fruits around the base to form a colourful mound. Top with a few handfuls of chestnuts.

hints
Submerge the ivy trails in water for 1 hour before use, especially if the candelabra will stand in a warm room. Decorate the candelabra in situ as it will be almost impossible to move later.

winter

▼ **Holly** (*Ilex*) Green holly leaves are a traditional and popular Christmas material. They are available all year round and form a stunning backdrop to their own red or white berries in the winter. They are long lasting and there are many varieties, including those with variegated leaves.

▼ **Chinese lanterns** (*Physalis*) The papery and delicate balloons that surround the small, golden coloured fruit closely resemble real Chinese lanterns. The deliciously sweet berries can be used to decorate seasonal wreaths and garlands or be added to floral arrangements.

▲ **Winterberry** (*Ilex verticillata*) This plant is a member of the holly family and the sprays of bright red berries borne on bare stems are a perfect way to add colour and form to an arrangement. Although they look like redcurrants, like all holly berries, they are poisonous.

▼ **Cranberries** Small edible berries such as cranberries can be used fresh or dried to add warmth, texture and luxurious colour to autumn and winter designs, especially table decorations.

▼ **Amaryllis** (*Hippeastrum*) Often grown as pot plants for Christmas, they are also wonderful as cut flowers, ideal to provide a dramatic focus to a Christmas arrangement. Choose from white, pink or luscious red, all big and bold.

▲ **Walnuts** The archetypal Christmas nuts are also useful in decorations as their wrinkled shells provide texture and interest. Arrange loose, glue or wire into position.

Winter frosts

The snow-white eucharis and silvery eucalyptus give this arrangement a delicate, lightly-frosted look, while the pussy willow introduces a note of fluffy softness and just a hint of colour. Choose a narrow-necked vase to give greater impact to the softly-spreading foliage.

Time to make: 15 minutes

what you need
SMALL BUNCH OF EUCHARIS
EUCALYPTUS FOLIAGE
SMALL BUNCH OF PUSSY WILLOW
SMOKED GLASS VASE
SECATEURS

preparing the stems
1. Half-fill the vase with water to which a little bleach has been added (see page 140). Strip the lower leaves from the eucalyptus stems and cut them to slightly different lengths. Gather a small bunch of willow stems in your hand, and add a few slightly shorter eucalyptus stems around them.

making up the bunch
2. Add more eucalyptus and willow stems to make a mixed bunch with a pleasing, rounded shape (see page 140). Trim off the bottom of the stems so they are level, and place the bunch into the vase. The lowest leaves should be close to the vase rim. Take out and retrim the stems if necessary.

adding colour
3. Trim the eucharis stems and add them to the arrangement, evenly spacing them to add colour on all sides. Vary the heights of the stems to add interest.

variation
Almost anything else could be used in place of the eucharis as the feature flowers. Try Paperwhite daffodils which come into flower in winter and have a sweet scent.

Pure and simple snowdrops

This living, natural arrangement allows you to enjoy the beauty of snowdrops without having to go out into the cold to do so. When the flowers die, move the pot to a cool position and keep the compost just moist. When the leaves die back in spring, plant the bulbs outside in a shady spot and new flowers will emerge next winter.

Time to make: 15 minutes

what you need
1 POT OF SNOWDROPS
SMALL STONE POT
WHITE GRAVEL
POTTING COMPOST

preparing the pot
1. Place a good handful of gravel in the bottom of the pot to act as a drainage layer. Add a good handful of compost on top and press down to firm lightly (see page 142).

planting the flowers
2. Slide the snowdrops out of their pot carefully, cupping the rootball in your hand to stop it falling apart. Lower the roots gently into the stone pot. The top of the rootball should be just below the rim of the pot. If necessary, remove the snowdrops and adjust the amount of compost.

filling up
3. Add more compost to the pot, firming it gently around the roots until the pot is full. Arrange a layer of gravel on top to cover the compost.

variation
Any small bulbs can be treated in this way. Choose from crocus, scillas, dwarf irises or miniature narcissi for a more colourful display.

Valentine orchid

This delicate yet dramatic orchid makes the ideal Valentine's day gift or table centrepiece. Moth orchids are surprisingly robust and this display should last for a long time, provided it is placed in a bright position and kept moist.

Time to make: 15 minutes

what you need

1 WHITE MOTH ORCHID
   (PHALAENOPSIS)
SQUARE GLASS TANK
LOVE HEART SWEETS
SCISSORS

trimming the pot

1. Remove the rim from the orchid pot with a sharp pair of scissors to make it less visible in the final display.

filling the tank

2. Place a few sweets in the bottom of tank and stand the the pot on top. This will keep the pot from standing in water on the base of the tank. Next fill up the spaces around the orchid pot with love heart sweets, right up to the rim of the tank. Arrange some of the sweets so they are facing outwards against the glass as you fill it.

variation

To add interest, you could decorate the stem or supporting stick of the orchid using a trail of ivy (below right), ribbon or raffia. Instead of sweets, try filling the tank with pebbles, pulses, glass beads or rice.

hints

Allow the orchid roots to lay across the top of the sweets as they are very attractive. Remember to keep the orchid compost moist at all times. Do not eat the sweets as they may be damp.

Hyacinth heaven

Hyacinths are traditional Christmas flowers. In this arrangement, the hyacinths are cut level and tightly massed into a modern glass tank. As these white flowers open, the sweet scent will be almost overwhelming. The dark green of the fern leaves provides the deeper tones necessary to make the display complete.

Time to make: 15 minutes

what you need
LARGE BUNCH OF HYACINTHS
4 FERN LEAVES
SQUARE GLASS TANK
SHARP KNIFE

preparing the flowers
1. Lay the hyacinths flat on a work surface and cut the stems all to the same length. Take as little as possible off the stems so that they keep a little of the bulb, as this will help them to last longer.

standing up straight
2. Fill the glass tank about one-third full with water to which a little bleach has been added (see page 140). Gather up the flowers and place them into the tank. The tank should be full enough to force the stems to stand upright, but don't jam the stems in too tight.

positioning the ferns
3. Cut the stems off the ferns and insert 1 leaf down each side of the vase against the glass on the inside. You may have to use a thin stick to help position them.

variation
Any bulbs with fleshy stems can be arranged in this way. Try tulips instead, or grape hyacinths (Muscari) for a smaller arrangement.

hint
Try to buy hyacinths with leaves for the best effect.

Midwinter berry basket

This seasonal basket is a twist on many of the elements of a traditional Christmas, incorporating Christmas trees, holly berries and the Star of Bethlehem. It will last right through the festive season, making a bright splash of colour in a living room, hallway and even the Christmas dinner table.

Time to make: 25 minutes

what you need

BLUE PINE FOLIAGE

WINTERBERRY (ILEX VERTICILLATA)

WALNUTS

PINE CONES

GOLD STAR DECORATIONS

BASKET

CELLOPHANE

SCISSORS

FLORIST'S FOAM

KNIFE

SECATEURS

preparing the basket
1. Line the basket with cellophane to make it fully watertight (see page 136). Cut pieces of foam to fit the basket and soak them in water until they are wet right through. Place the foam in the basket and cut off the excess cellophane around the edges. Cut the pine foliage into small sprigs and strip the lower needles off the stems, then insert them into the foam.

making up the dome
2. Continue to add pieces of pine until you have built up a full dome of foliage. Angle the lower pieces straight out horizontally at the sides.

adding colour
3. Trim the winterberry into smaller pieces and insert sprigs throughout the pine foliage, spacing them evenly. Turn the basket frequently to check that they are all evenly distributed.

finishing touches
4. Insert a few gold stars to add interest, then place a few walnuts and pine cones amongst the foliage, pushing them back into it to hold them in place.

Dreamy orchids

For this serene arrangement, I've created an atmosphere of heaven on earth for the bedroom. The pure and delicate beauty of the white orchids, combined with the earthy terracotta of the roof tiles and the freshness of green bear grass, results in the perfect setting for dreaming.

Time to make: 15 minutes

what you need

3 WHITE MOTH ORCHID STEMS
   (PHALAENOPSIS)
SMALL BUNCH OF BEAR GRASS
SMALL VASE
2 CURVED TUSCAN ROOF TILES
COCO FIBRE TWINE
SCISSORS

preparing the vase

1. Half-fill the vase with water, place it between the roof tiles and push them together. (The vase must be small enough so the tiles will close-up around it.)

binding the tiles

2. Bind the tiles together with coco twine and secure with a bow. Trim off the loose ends of the twine.

adding the flowers

3. Arrange the orchids and bear grass in the vase. Fan the bear grass slightly so that it arches naturally over the sides of the tiles.

Variation

Substitute the roof tiles with small bamboo poles cut to size and arrange them around the small vase. Secure the bamboo with coco fibre twine to create an exotic eastern look.

Christmas fruit basket

A modern take on a traditional Christmas gift, with exotic and tropical fruit and leaves to suit your taste. The banana leaf should dry well in position, making an attractive permanent addition to this festive basket.

Time to make: 25 minutes

what you need

SEASONAL FRUIT AND NUTS
BANANA LEAF
BASKET WITH HANDLE
RAFFIA
COCO FIBRE TWINE
SCISSORS

the basic frame
1. Take a handful of raffia and wind the strands into a neat circle. Place the raffia in the bottom of the basket. Cut 2 long strips from the banana leaf and place them in the bottom of the basket, arranged in a cross, with the ends protruding above the basket rim.

arranging the fruit
2. Arrange the fruit in the basket, with the larger fruit on the bottom and smaller fruit on top. Try to group them by variety.

topping up
3. Save a few physalis for the top of the basket as they have an interesting shape.

decorating the basket
4. Decorate the basket by wrapping a deep band of banana leaf around the outside and securing it with coco twine. Cut a thin strip of banana leaf and twist it around the handle of the basket, securing it at either end with a shorter piece tied in a knot.

hint
Choose a wide selection of exotic fruits for this seasonal gift. Mangosteens, figs, lychees, kumquats, physalis, cranberries, dates and walnuts always make a welcome treat.

Cyclamen crate

A sturdy wooden crate has been transformed into an effective planter, filled with long-flowering cyclaman, dainty mind-your-own-business and handsome ivy. Here, foliage is the key, with a stunning mix of textures and subtle colours, all carefully packed with moss.

Time to make: 45 minutes

what you need

2 LARGE WHITE-FLOWERED
    CYCLAMEN PLANTS
10–12 MIND-YOUR-OWN-BUSINESS
    (SOLEIROLIA) PLANTS
4–6 IVIES
LARGE WOODEN BOX
POLYSTYRENE OR OTHER LIGHT-
    WEIGHT DRAINAGE MATERIAL
PLASTIC SHEETING
SCISSORS
POTTING COMPOST
MOSS

preparing the box

1. Line the box with plastic, leaving the edges overlapping the sides of the box (see page 136). Break the polystyrene into chunks and make a deep layer in the bottom of the box for drainage.

2. Pour a deep layer of compost into the box on top of the polystyrene. Firm it down well, then add more if necessary until it is 15 cm (6 inches) below the box rim.

planting the flowers

3. Remove the cyclamen from their pots and lower the rootballs into the compost in the middle of the box (see page 142). Add more compost around their roots to bring the level up to about 10 cm (4 inches) below the box rim. Remove the ivies from their pots and plant in the corners of the box with the foliage hanging out over the edges.

4. Fill in the spaces around the cyclamen with mind-your-own-business plants, planting them in the same way and alternating the colours. The aim is to cover the compost entirely with the foliage.

filling the gaps

5. Firm the compost between the roots of the plants and add more compost to fill any gaps. Trim the excess plastic from around the box edges and water the compost well. Cover any bare compost with moss, tucking it into corners and between plants. Fill any holes in the sides of the box with moss, too.

hints

A plastic sack or bin liner is suitable to line the box, as long as it does not have any holes in it.
Polystyrene plant pot trays can be broken into chunks for drainage material.

Fresh and festive garland

A mantlepiece provides the perfect foil for a seasonal garland. This garland will last through the holiday season and the versatile design can be easily adapted by changing the fruit or ribbon, adding a few favourite family baubles or some fresh seasonal flowers.

Time to make: 45 minutes

what you need
BLUE PINE BRANCHES
HOLLY WITH BERRIES
DRIED LOTUS PODS
DRIED CLEMENTINES
SILVER RIBBON
REEL WIRE
STUB WIRES
WIRE CUTTERS
SECATEURS

the basic garland

1. Cut the blue pine into small sprigs, roughly 20 cm (8 inches) long. Arrange 1 sprig on top of another, facing in the same direction but slightly offset and wire them together by wrapping reel wire around the stems (see page 138). Do not cut the wire off the reel, keep it attached. Add another sprig on top of the first 2, again slightly offset but facing in the same direction and bind in place with the wire. Continue to add sprigs in the same way to make a garland. Continue until the garland is just over half the length of your mantlepiece, then cut the wire off the reel. Make another garland in the same way, then join the 2 together by wiring them securely at their stem ends.

attaching the holly

2. Attach a stub wire (see page 138) to each piece of holly by winding it round the stem; leave the ends long.

3. Use the wire ends to attach the holly sprigs to the garland, spacing them equally along its length.

adding the fruits

4. Start wiring the dried clementines together in groups by passing the wire through the skins, then attach them to the garland using the wire ends. Wire the lotus pods in position in the same way.

5. Attach a stub wire to the back of a ribbon bow and fix it to the centre of the garland.

variation

Vary the fruits and other decorations according to your colour scheme, but don't overdo it or the garland will look like a fruit basket.

hint

The dried clementines are quite heavy so attach them securely or arrange them so that that they sit flat on top of the pine.

Spiky Christmas tree

A great alternative to a traditional Christmas tree, this simple design is remarkably effective, and will be a talking point in any room. Position against a plain background to appreciate it to the full.

Time to make: 25 minutes

what you need
LARGE BRANCHING CACTUS
    IN A POT
FRESH RED CHILLIES ON STEMS
LARGE TERRACOTTA POT
PEBBLES
FAIRY LIGHTS

the basic shape
1. Place the cactus, still in its pot, inside the terracotta pot. Place a deep layer of large pebbles on top to cover the inner pot.

attaching the lights
2. Carefully wind the fairy lights around the cactus, taking care not to prick your fingers. Try to arrange the lights so that they are evenly spaced and point outwards from the cactus to make them more visible. Use the cactus spines to hold the wires in place.

adding colour
3. Trim the stems of the chillies and attach them all over the cactus, using the light wires to hold the stems in place.

hints
Make the whole arrangement in situ as it will be too heavy, and very spiky, to move afterwards. Remember to position it close enough to a power socket.
Wash your hands after handling the chillies as they can irritate the eyes if you touch them afterwards.

Cool as ice

What could be more beautiful than an ice creation in the softly-glowing candle light of a special winter meal or Christmas celebration? Decorated with just a few simple holly leaves and cranberries, the increasing depths of beautiful colour become visible in the ice as it slowly melts.

Time to make: 45 minutes

what you need

HOLLY LEAVES
CRANBERRIES
ICE BLOCK
CANDLESTICK (ICE IF POSSIBLE)
WIDE GLASS DISH
NIGHT LIGHT OR CANDLE
HAMMER

preparing the ice

1. Place the candlestick in the middle of the dish. Smash up the block of ice with a hammer into small pieces and place them in the dish around the candlestick.

adding colour

2. Decorate the bowl of ice with holly leaves and cranberries, allowing some to drop down between the chunks of ice.

lighting up

3. Place the night light or the candle in the top of the candlestick and light it.

hints

To get very clear ice chunks, make the ice using distilled water as tap water will make cloudy ice. Freeze it in a large plastic container.
Any candlestick will do, but an ice one will be the most effective. Ask an ice maker to make you one, if possible, or make your own. Use a tall plastic cylinder or vase as a mould. Mould a piece of plasticine into a shape just larger than a night light. Press it firmly on to the base of the dry mould. Gently add the distilled water and freeze. When frozen, dip the mould briefly in warm water to remove the candlestick and the plasticine.
Make this as late as possible before displaying as it will start to melt quite quickly. Keep your eye on it as the water will eventually over-flow the dish as it melts.

techniques

Working with foam

cutting foam
1. First cut the foam roughly down to size with a sharp knife, so that it is a bit larger than the container. Always place the foam on a flat surface to cut it in order to avoid hurting yourself if the knife slips. Use more than one piece of foam in a large display, cutting them to size if necessary.

soaking
2. Place the foam in a large bowl of clean water. It is ready to use when it sinks, indicating that it is wet right through. Lift it out and let the free water run off.

trying for fit
3. Check the shape of the foam against the container and trim off any corners that will not squash down.

squashing it home
4. The point of using foam is to hold the stems tightly in position, so the foam needs to be squashed down very firmly into the container, to ensure a tight fit.

variation
If you are using foam inside a non-watertight container, such as a wicker basket, first line the container with plastic or cellophane, then add the wet foam. Finally, trim the cellophane so that it is not visible above the rim of the container.

hints
Thick stems will slide into foam more easily if cut on the diagonal.
When working with foam, try to avoid repositioning stems too much as the foam is likely to break up.

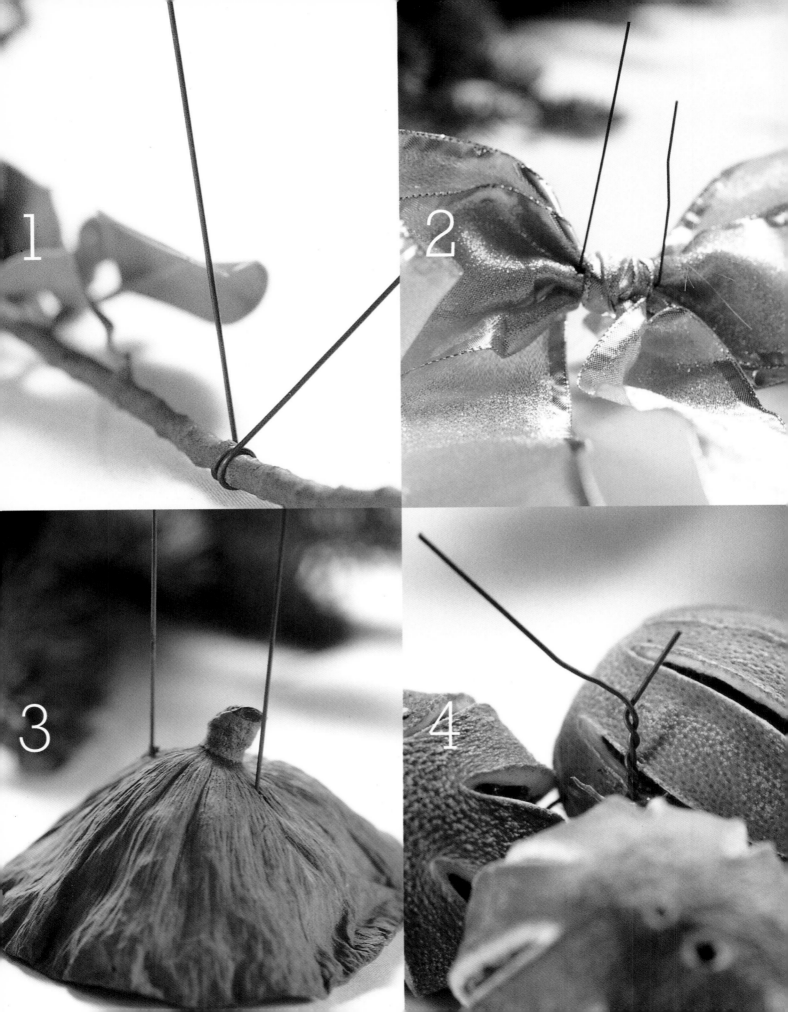

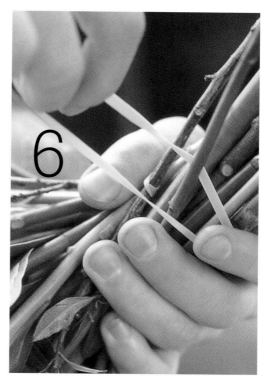

Wiring and securing

Wire is available in two forms. Reel wire is fine wire, wound onto a reel and is used for binding and making wreaths and garlands. Stub wires are short, straight lengths of thicker wire, used for wiring materials on to wreaths and garlands.

wiring a stem
1. Hold the wire at right angles to the stem. Wrap the wire round the stem evenly and smoothly, leaving the two ends even and long.

wiring ribbon
2. Tie a bow in a piece of ribbon, thread a stub wire through the knot at the back and bend the ends parallel to each other.

wiring seedheads
3. Push a length of stub wire through the seedhead, just above the stem. Bend the ends of the wire parallel to each other and use them to attach the seedhead to a wreath or garland.

joining objects
4. Some materials look best when they are arranged in a group. Thread a straight piece of wire through the first object, such as a dried clementine. Bend it a little and thread it through the next item. Repeat this, and when all the objects are joined, twist the ends of the wire together. Use the loose ends to fix the wired fruits on to a garland.

rubber bands
A rubber band provides a simple means of securing a bunch of woody stems, such as roses, together.
5. Hook one end of the band over one or two of the rose stems to hold it in place.

6. Wrap the other end right around the bunch until it is tight, then hook it over another stem to hold it firm.

Arranging tips

preparing flowers

All flowers should be put in water before you work with them, especially shop-bought stems which will have dried out on the way home.
Cut off about 2.5 cm (1 inch) from the bottom of the stems using secateurs or a sharp knife.
One exception to this rule is hyacinths. If a part of the fleshy bulb is left at the end of the stem, do not cut it off. It contains food and will help the flowers to last longer.
If flowers such as tulips have drooped, they must be supported with the stems erect to absorb water. Lay the blooms in an even row on a piece of newspaper. Trim the stem ends evenly. Roll the flowers up in the newspaper into a very straight sausage and plunge the bottoms into water for at least an hour.

preventing rot

When preparing flowers for a display, remove any lower leaves that will be below the water level to avoid them rotting when submerged. To prevent algae making the water cloudy in displays in clear glass vases, add bleach to the water – about an eggcup per pint is enough.

lily pollen

To avoid lily pollen staining furniture or your clothes, remove the stamens before you arrange them.

a perfect bouquet

The aim of arranging a perfect hand-held bouquet is to show off the flower heads at their best, with all of them facing outwards. Start with a few flowers to act as a central core. Simply hold these together in your hand. Start to add stems around this central core, arranging them at a slight angle, all leaning in the same direction. You will eventually have built up a neat spiral around the central core stems. Add further layers around the outside, still leaning in the same direction and staggering the stems between the existing stems. When the bouquet is complete, you will note that the bottoms of the stems fan out in a neat spiral and the tops form a softly-rounded mound.

water phials

Some cut flowers, such as orchids and gerberas, are sold with their stems in a small phial of liquid. If they are destined for a waterless display, simply top it up with water. Otherwise, snip the phial off carefully and trim the stem as usual.

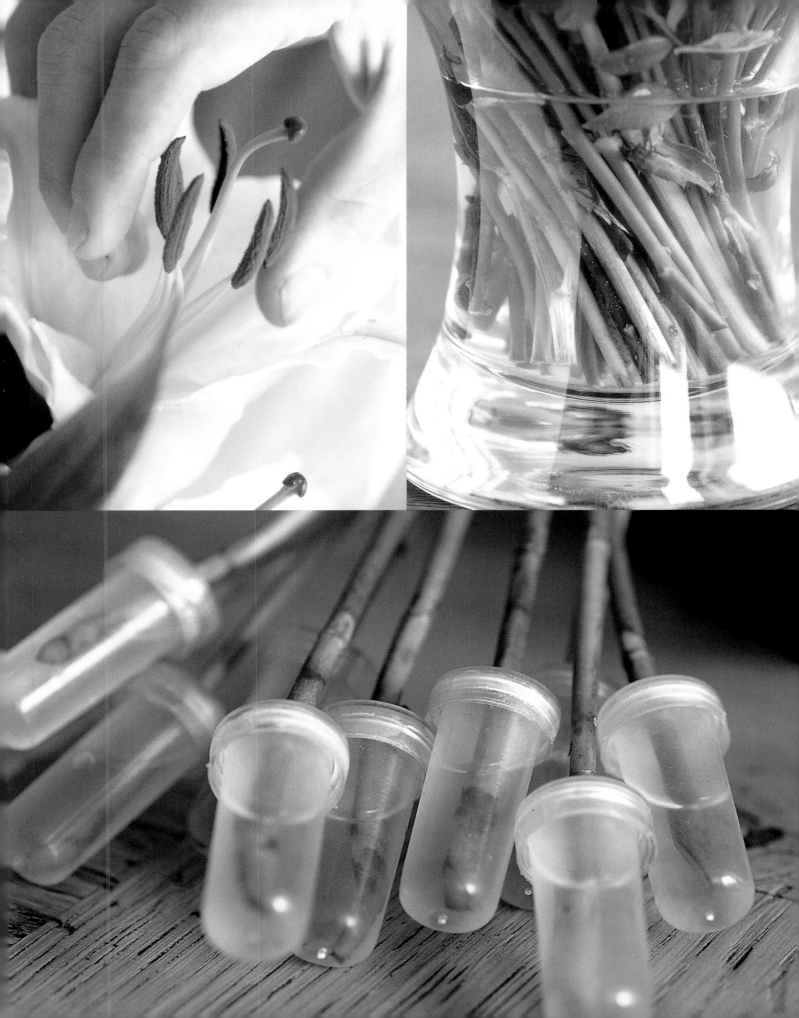

Living plants

Plants, as well as cut flowers, make great subjects for interesting displays.

soaking first

Always soak potted plants in water for at least an hour before you take them out of their pots. This will moisten the compost, allowing them to soak up moisture more easily after they have been transplanted.

compost

Most plants are happy in a general potting compost, especially if the display is a temporary one, but some, such as cacti and orchids, have specific requirements about such things as drainage and acidity. Check with your supplier as to which compost is best for the plants you wish to use.

pot size

Avoid giving flowering plants too much space when you transplant them. They will produce lots of roots and be shy to flower.

drainage

If there are no drainage holes in the bottom of the pot, add a layer of gravel, rocks or chunks of polystyrene before you add the compost. This will allow excess water to settle underneath this layer, preventing the compost above becoming waterlogged.

repotting

Put any necessary drainage material in the bottom of the new pot. Add enough compost so that when the plant sits on it, the top of the rootball is just below the rim of the pot. Fill around the plant with compost and firm it down gently with your fingers. Water the plant in thoroughly once you have finished.

index